FUERTEVEN ROAD TI

ALL ROADS LEAD TO DISCOVERING
FUERTEVENTURA'S HIDDEN GEMS

Stephen Cartledge

©2022 Stephen Cartledge. All rights reserved.

No part of this publication mat be reproduced, or transmitted in any form by any means, electronic, mechanical, photocopying, recording, scanning or otherwise, without the prior written permission from the Author, except for the use of brief quotations in a book review and certain other noncommercial uses permitted by copyright law.

For permission requests, contact the Author at :-

stepheninfo9@gmail.com

Date of publication :- 06/09/2022

Printed by Amazon

   Since 2020

ISBN : 9798849934310

Stephen Cartledge
296/ M12 Phan Prao
Ampheo Si Chiang Mai
Nong Khai. Thailand.

+66 0909591958

Fuerteventura is much more than just the sea, sun, and sandy beaches.
On this side of the paradise, you will find beautiful villages with all kinds of heritage.

FUERTEVENTURA ROAD TRIP	1
LET'S DISCOVER	6
GETTING TO KNOW THE ROADS	10
THE NORTHERN ROUTE	14
NR-1 The Parque Natural de las Dunas de Corralejo	15
NR-2 Lajares	17
NR-3 El Cotillo	19
NR-4 Corralejo	21
NR-5 Lobos	22
THE CENTRAL ROUTE	26
CR-1 Antigua	27
CR-2 Betancuria	30
CR-3 Ajuy	36
THE SOUTHERN ROUTE	42
SR-1 Montaña del Cardón.	43
SR-2 La Pared	46
SR-3 Cofete	51
SR-4 Puerto de la Cruz	58

SR-5 La Lajita, (Oasis Park). 62

IMPORTANT INFO FOR DRIVING IN SPAIN 69

IN CASE OF EMERGENCY 74

EXPLORING BY BUS 75

FERRY FROM FUERTEVENTURA TO
LANZAROTE 88

author note 91

LET'S DISCOVER

We all know Fuerteventura for it's Kilometres of heavenly white or golden sand beaches with turquoise waters, but there is much more to this Island once we get out and discover the interior.

I will take you through the heart and lungs of the second largest island in the archipelago, on some of the not to miss routes. Let's forget about sunbathing all day, and get out and explore some secret and unusual places this amazing island has to offer. There are so many places hidden away from the popular tourist routes, you will get to see another side of Fuerteventura, one which is wild and unexplored.

So if you are looking for hidden gems and secret places, in Fuerteventura, the best way to start your discoveries, is on the road by car.

Before we rush off, here are a few tips-

Driving is on the right in the Canary Islands. You may be allowed to overtake slow moving traffic on the left on some motorways and toll roads. Don't obstruct the fast lane or you will risk being undertaken. Buses and taxis will expect you to give way to them.

Remember ! you drive on the RIGHT SIDE here in Fuerteventura.

TRAFFIC LAWS

URBAN SPEED LIMIT
50 kph

More info

RURAL SPEED LIMIT
100 kph

More info

MOTORWAY SPEED LIMIT
120 kph

More info

DRINK DRIVE LIMIT
30-50mg

More info

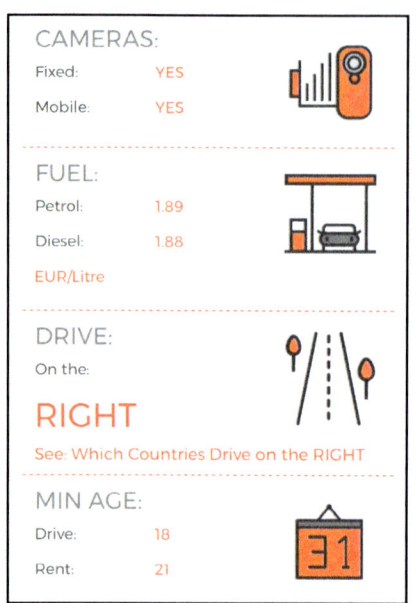

CAMERAS:
Fixed: YES
Mobile: YES

FUEL:
Petrol: 1.89
Diesel: 1.88
EUR/Litre

DRIVE:
On the:
RIGHT
See: Which Countries Drive on the RIGHT

MIN AGE:
Drive: 18
Rent: 21

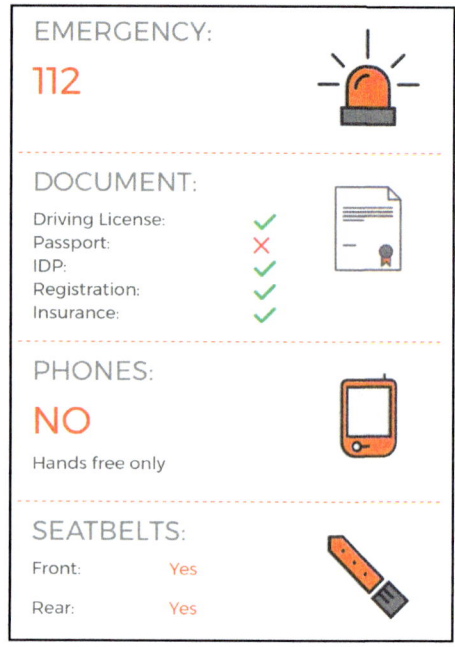

EMERGENCY:
112

DOCUMENT:
Driving License: ✓
Passport: ✗
IDP: ✓
Registration: ✓
Insurance: ✓

PHONES:
NO
Hands free only

SEATBELTS:
Front: Yes
Rear: Yes

Traffic violations sanctioned in the Road Safety Act must always be paid.
If you are informed of the fine when the violation is committed, it can be paid on the spot. If it is not possible to pay it, the Civil Guard may impound the vehicle until it is paid.

Welcome to paradise, where the magic begins and memories last a life time.

GETTING TO KNOW THE ROADS

The main roads are FV-1 (Puerto del Rosario to Corralejo) and FV-2 (Puerto del Rosario to Morro Jable), and are pretty well maintained. The FV-3 runs around the capital city of puerto del Rosario from the FV-2 before joining the FV-1.
If this is your first time you've driven in Fuerteventura, don't panic, like i said earlier all the roads are pretty much well maintained so you're in for a comfortable ride.
Other major roads on the island are the FV-10 which runs from the north and continues through the center of the island from El Cotillo right down to Puerto del Rosario, passing through some incredible places listed below.

- El Rogue
- Malpais de la Areaa
- La Oliva
- Tindaya
- La Matilla
- Tamariche

Next we can pick up the FV-101 from the FV-1 outside of Corralejo and journey on to the village of Villaverde and La Oliva.
Heading south out of the capital, Puerto del Rosario, pick up the FV-20 taking you in-land before dropping south before picking up FV-4 to Gran Tarajal.
Towns and villages on route include:-

- La Ampuyenta

- Antigua
- Velles de Ortega
- Tuineje

Betancuria and Pajara are reached by driving on the FV-30. So you can see there are many road options when driving North to South of the island if you decide to go quick and direct by using the FV-1 FV-2 or the scenic routes using the FV-20 - FV-30 and FV-4.

Handy Phrases

- Give way - Ceda el paso
- Right of way – Prioridad
- Exit – Salida
- Danger – Peligro
- No parking - Prohibido aparcar
- Slow – Despacio
- Lane – Un carril
- City centre – Centro ciudad
- Roadworks – Obras
- Excuse me, I'm lost – Por favor, estoy perdido…
- Go straight on – 'Siga todo recto'
- Turn right – 'Toma el giro a la derecha'
- Turn left – 'Toma el giro a la izquierda'
- Detour - Desviacion
- Road Closed – Cerrado.
- Road Open – Abierto
- One way street – Direccíon unica

MAJOR ROADS

APPROX TRAVEL TIME

THE NORTHERN ROUTE

All the routes on our island discovery, will start out of Caleta de Fuste, but you can pick up the route from your own destination by following the appropriate FV routes.
We start on the FV-2 for a 50 minute and a 44 km drive.

Head towards Puerto del Rosario before continuing our journey north towards Corralejo with a must see stop off at the parque natural de corralejo, (sand dunes). I have spoken about this area in my first book titled, "Fuerteventura" but i'll give a brief description for the first timers to the island.

NR-1 The Parque Natural de las Dunas de Corralejo

FV-1 ROUTE

Is one of the most-visited natural areas in Fuerteventura and boasts the largest sand dunes of the Canary Islands. With miles of near white sand beaches, clear turquoise waters, huge dunes and a contrasting red and black volcanic landscape, it is a real natural gem of the Canary Islands. The Natural Park covers around 24 km², including the beaches, the large shifting sand dunes and the volcanic landscape to the south. Known locally as Grandes Playas (big beaches), the 10 Km stretch of coastline is actually made up of a number of smaller beaches. These pale sandy beaches have few rocks and clear turquoise waters. Contrary to many guides and newspaper articles, the sand here has not "blown over from the Sahara", but is in fact composed of the shells of marine creatures. My personal opinion, is, this is one gem you must not miss.

After a short break on the white sandy dunes we will continue north but turn off on to the FV-109 in the direction of Lajares. 28 minute and 17.7 km drive.

NR-2 Lajares

Lajares sits just 6.4 km from the center of El Cotillo. Most people just drive straight through Lajares without even giving it a glance. I was fortunate enough to rent my first house here so i know what this area has to offer.
The area's natural wilderness offers a great variety of hiking options. Dozens of trails crisscross one another amid volcanoes and even beaches to form a great network. The most popular and suitable for all types of people is the Calderón Hondo Volcano trail, a circular path spanning just over five kilometres.

From the summit, a enormous 70 meter deep crater and panoramic views of the island's northern coast can be seen. After a nice walk of discovery, why not head back to the square. Lajares is a great place to get to know the Canary Islands' most deep-rooted customs and traditions. In the heart of the village all kinds of items are handcrafted: silk, jewellery, hats, leather, paintings, soap and, of course, the finest variety of culinary produce. Be sure to try the Majorero cheese, which you won't be able to resist. In addition to picturesque shops and crafts markets, the centre of the village is home to countless workshops where artisans hone their creativity. Every Saturday, from 10:00 AM to 2:00 PM, a traditional market takes place on the village square, in which shops, workshops and artists exhibit their items steeped in history. I would recommend taking a leisurely stroll through the market and learning about the techniques and people behind these unique products.

Again i would highly recommend stopping off here, get on your hiking shoes and head for Calderón Hondo, you will not be disappointed with the spectacular views and, the stunning photo opportunities.

CALDERON HONDO

Back in the car now for a short drive down in to El Cotillo.

NR-3 El Cotillo

Once you enter the coastal village of El Cotillo, you will find a series of family friendly coves of white sand and calm turquoise waters. La Concha beach is one of the best known in Fuerteventura for its beauty, quality and tranquillity. The beach's close proximity to the town allows you to enjoy a break with incredible sea views and amazing sunsets, where the sky changes from ochre to violet in a matter of minutes.

La Concha beach is approximately 220 m in length and enjoys gentle waves thanks to its natural horseshoe-shaped reef. When the wind picks up the 'corralitos', small circular walls made from volcanic rock built by residents, are the perfect refuge, and at low tide the smallest members of the family can play safely in the small rock pools that form. There is parking very close to the beach and a lifeguard service as well as apartments and a restaurant nearby.

After some time spent at the lagoons, take a walk through the village in El Cotillo besides its amazing beaches, this place will not disappoint. You can see how it has preserved its fishing tradition over the years: from its small harbor filled with colourful boats, to the wharf filled with seafood restaurants.

Every day, the fishermen unload the fishes freshly caught, which are then prepared by the many restaurants. Make sure to check out one of them during your visit to El Cotillo.

Just a 7 minute drive up the coast and a distance of 3.4 km, you will find one of the most famous monuments in El Cotillo - the Tostón lighthouse. It was built in the 19th century to mark the Strait of Bocaina, which is the strait between the islands of Fuerteventura and Lanzarote. Formerly a wonderful lighthouse that has now been converted into a museum, for a good sunset, this place is perfect, as it combines the sea, the coves and the lighthouse in one panoramic view.

CONCHA BEACH

COTILLO SUNSET

Driving out of El Cotillo on the FV-10, then at the roundabout take the first exit on to the FV-109 Lajares. Continue on this route until you reach the FV-1 towards Corralejo, this is our stop over night.

NR-4 Corralejo

Explore the many bars or spend a night with live music in the square. The vibe at this quaint square in Corralejo, feels like going back years to a past time where people actually talked, danced and dined together. Well worth spending a night out here.

MUSIC SQUARE CORRALEJO

We can either take a short drive or walk to the harbour front, from it's here we will take a 15 minute boat ride across to the island of Los Lobos.

NR-5 Lobos

Lobos is a small unspoiled island a few kilometers north of Fuerteventura. Wild nature, volcanic wilderness and authentic beauty – this is Lobos, an island that takes its name from the old sea lions that used to inhabit its coastline.

The island is rich in ecology, which led to it being declared a protected area and being designated as a Natural Park. In addition, its rich seabed has been declared as an underwater reserve. Its highest point is La Caldera at 127 m. Its 13 km of coastline and 4 km² area are full of small beaches and coves, enormous sandbanks, solidified lava rivers and malpaises.

Permits

Since 2019, access to Lobos has been limited by Fuerteventura's government to ensure the sustainability of the natural spaces. The permit is free, however, you are only able to reserve it 5 days before your visit. You can only get a permit for a maximum of 3 people. It also limits your time on the island to just 4 hours:

Morning hours (10am-2pm)

Afternoon hours (2pm-6pm)

Looking around Lobos

As soon as you step off the boat, you can contemplate the island's natural purity. There is just an information cabin and a statue in memory of the sea lions that used to populate the island. 4 km2 of wild nature and spectacular untouched wilderness is waiting for us. Most people who visit the island do so to enjoy the magnificent coves and beaches, but the small size of the island means you can enjoy the coast as well as taking a walk through its trails.

The trails are well defined, and the points of interest are perfectly signposted. Lobos has been declared a protected area, so it is forbidden to leave the paths to maintain the purity of the island. If you're planning on walking on any of them, it's recommended to wear suitable shoes and protect yourself from the sun that looms over the island practically all year round.

The main route starts in the southern area, where we disembark and traverse the whole island through the centre

ISLAND OF LOBOS

towards the lighthouse on the north coast, from which you can see the south face of Lanzarote.

The first thing that draws the attention when you start the route is the La Caldera volcano, which is the highest point of Lobos at 127 m and what initially created the island. You can climb to the summit, and as well as the crater you'll be able to delight in the privileged views towards Lanzarote and the Sand Dunes of Corralejo (Dunas de Corralejo).

On Lobos, there is only one restaurant, so if you want to make sure you have food, it's recommended to make a reservation there as soon as you arrive on the island, or even bring your own food.

Bathing areas

There are several beaches and coves on Lobos Island, but because it is a protected area, access is only allowed to El Puertito. The rest of the beaches have restricted access.

La Concha Beach (Playa de La Concha), also known as La Caleta Beach (Playa de La Caleta) is found in the south of Lobos. It is a rocky white sand beach, with a horseshoe shape and fairly wide.

Very close, to the east of La Concha, you'll find El Puertito, a spectacular cove with crystal-clear waters that is ideal for snorkeling. A visit to the island of Lobos is a must see gem on this Northern route.

THE CENTRAL ROUTE

Heading out of Caleta de Fuste on FV-2 towards the airport, at the roundabout you will see the sign for FV- 413. Take this route for our first stop of the day in, Antigua. 16 minutes, 18.4 km drive.

CR-1 Antigua

Antigua is a village in Fuerteventura, which is the capital of the region of Antigua.

It is a historic village, founded by European colonisers that established it there to take advantage of the productive land for cultivation. Antigua soon became prominent among the local population thanks to its strategic location between Villa de Betancuria and the docks on the island's west coast.

The village is dominated by the arid landscapes that characterise inland Fuerteventura. A visit is highly recommended thanks to its historic importance and the beauty of its architectural heritage.

Places of interest in Antigua

Iglesia de Antigua. The main catholic church in the village which has stood since the 16th-century, when it was a small chapel. Over the following centuries, it was remodelled various times until it took its current shape.

Casa del Portón. Old statement home constructed in the 17th century. It is notable for its many elements of traditional Canarian architecture. It current homes the Antigua Municipal Library.

Molinos de Antigua. The windmills were at their peak in Fuerteventura during the 18th century and were mainly dedicated to extracting water and milling grain, which made the island the breadbasket of the Canary Islands.

The windmills that have survived over the centuries reveal the history of their practice.

Majorero Cheese Museum. This unique museum enlightens us about the origin and manufacture of the most popular cheese in Fuerteventura. This industry has had a huge impact on the life and even the landscapes of the island.

I would again highly recommend you don't leave without sampling the cheese.

ANTIGUA VILLAGE

ANTIGUA CHEESE MUSEUM

Near Antigua, you'll find places like Villa de Betancuria, which has the most beautiful centre on the island, or the Betancuria Rural Park, one of the most distinctive natural spaces on the island.
Heading north out of Antigua we take route FV-416 before reaching our first roundabout and exiting to the FV-30.

The journey from Antigua to our next destination, Betancuria, is only 10.2 km west and about a 10 minute drive away.

CR-2 Betancuria

Fuerteventura is an island full of surprises that always manages to astonish with places steeped in history. One such place is Betancuria, the least-populated town on the Canary Island and was the islands former capitol city. The town's population of around 800 inhabitants holds onto the memory of its foundation, by Jean Béthencourt, in the fifteenth century.

Its location in the valley of Macizo de Betancuria is, in part, responsible for its success as a tourist destination. In fact, it is considered the most important town, in an artistic sense, in Fuerteventura. Despite not having long beaches or important monuments, each year it attracts thousands of tourists who surrender to its charm. The main tourist attractions in Betancuria are linked to its unique nature, enjoying the authentic local cuisine and, above all, local peoples' hospitality towards visitors. Some of the islands must-visit places include Betancuria Rural Park, Guise viewpoint, the Archaeological Museum and the church of Santa María.

The brownish colours of the terrain of Betancuria Rural Park are, without a doubt, its main feature and the natural space is of great scientific interest. Its crags and massifs are home to countless protected plant species, such as nicotiana glauca, which is sometimes mixed with lower quality tobacco. A great variety of fauna can also be seen around the damns of Las Peñitas and Los Molinos, as well as around the cliffs, which serve as a refuge for the area's birds of prey.

The Betancuria massif has been the setting of important scientific findings, such as those concerning oceanic sediment and marine animal fossils. Be sure not to miss the Natural Monument of Ajuy, which is home to the oldest rocks in the whole archipelago.

The flora that lives in the crags and massifs also deserves some of your time, as it includes species endemic to

Fuerteventura, such as the balsam spurge, apteranthes buchardii and the Canary Island daisy. Palm trees and tamarix canariensis, trees that have been documented since the fifteenth century, also form part of the landscape.

Two large statues of the ancient kings of Fuerteventura preside over the landscape of the Guise viewpoint. The statues were not placed there at random, but rather recall how the island of Fuerteventura was divided into two kingdoms led by two monarchs in the fifteenth century. In this case, the sculptures represent Guise and Ayose. If you stand level with them, you'll be able to enjoy immense panoramic views of a desert landscape ranging in colour from ochre to yellow.

Archaeology and Ethnography Museum, Betancuria

A must-visit on any trip to Fuerteventura is the Archaeology Museum in Betancuria, which is housed within a pretty house built in traditional Canarian style right in the city centre.

The museum comprises three rooms, two of which are chiefly dedicated to archaeological pieces, whilst the last room centres on ethnographic objects. Although said spaces are fascinating, the exhibition that attracts the most interest is the one explaining the history of the first European expeditions to the Canary Islands, the way of life of inhabitants at the time, and their culture.

Another must-visit in Fuerteventura is the famous church of Santa María, which was founded in the fifteenth century as a small chapel to serve the religious needs of the island's inhabitants. Despite its size, it was the first cathedral in Fuerteventura. Of particular note in the place of worship, which consists of three naves separated by round arches, is the square tower built by Pedro de Párraga. Be sure to look out for its lovely Renaissance-inspired façade.

Moreover, the parish house also houses a museum exhibiting paintings and sculptures from other churches in Fuerteventura. The great historical importance of the town of Betancuria can be discovered at every turn, although it might be worth visiting some specific places, such as the remains of the convent of Saint Bonaventure, the first convent to be founded in the Canary Islands. In the monastery lived Franciscan monks who not only helped disseminate the religion but were a source of assistance and support for local people. The convent was also the burial site of an illustrious figure, Don Claudio de Lila, who was a royal engineer.

After exploring its natural spaces, landscapes and monuments, you'll no doubt attest to the fact that the small town of Betancuria is full of history, mystical places and restaurants that will provide you with unforgettable memories.

BETANCURIA MASSIF

Leaving Betancuria on route FV-30 we will pass through the village of Pajara.

I will give it a short mention for those who wish to stop to visit the church, Iglesia de Nuestra Señora de Regla. The church was built between 1687 and 1712. It is rather intriguing, with an Aztec-style stone facade, depicting the sun and moon, snakes eating their own tails and big cats (cougars or jaguars). This Mexican-inspired facade clearly differs from the usual baroque design of most churches on the island. It is believed that a local, returning from "the New World" influenced the unusual carvings. Inside, the church features some highly decorative retablos, which can be illuminated by placing a coin into the machine by the door. The church is best viewed in the afternoon sun, which lights up the stone facade.

Just across the road from the Church Square are several Bars and Cafes, which make for a great "rest-stop" while exploring the island. Here you can sample some local home-made cakes as well as tapas and other nibbles before continuing on. A local festival, the fiesta de Nuestra Señora de Regla, takes place every August, with around 15 days of events and activities.

Leaving Pajara on the FV- 605 before joining the FV-621 for a distance of 7.1 km, 12 minute drive.

CR-3 Ajuy

If you're looking for somewhere calm away from the main tourist centres on the island, this is the place to be. Ajuy is a small and welcoming fishing village on the western coast of Fuerteventura, mainly known for the unique caves in the mountains which surround it, and its fantastic volcanic black sand beach.

What's more, in Ajuy you can try the wonderful Canarian cuisine in the unrivalled restaurants along its shoreline. Tasting these magnificent dishes while immersed in the tranquil aura of the village and the horizon in front of your eyes is priceless.

The area just north of Ajuy village is a protected natural area of geological interest (Monumento Natural de Ajuy) because of its layers of ancient sedimentary rocks and fossils of extinct marine creatures. The Monumento Natural is situated within the larger Rural Park of Betancuria and is also a Special Protection Area for Birds.

A short coastal trail, which leads to the sea caves, begins at the northern end of the beach. Here you can clearly see the oldest rocks in the Canary Islands – over 100 million years old, formed before the American and African plates separated, along with layers of ancient beaches and deposits from long-dried up rivers. There is a great information board that is well worth taking the time to read before starting your walk. Sturdy shoes are recommended for this route.

The sea caves of Ajuy are the most spectacular on the island and often photographed. Along with the walking trail from the main beach, you can access to caves via the dirt road on the cliffs, though care should be taken getting down to the caves. Legend has it that pirates, that once plagued the islands, used the caves to store their loot.

A NOTE FOR SWIMMERS! THERE ARE SOME VERY STRONG CURRENTS IN THIS AREA, SO PLEASE BE CAUTIOUS.

Up until the second half of the 19th Century, limestone was quarried, shipped out and processed locally into quicklime in large kilns which are still visible on the main coastal walking route. The limestone from this area was considered to be of superior quality, though these industries have long since ceased operation in the area. Syenite cobblestones used in various locations in Gran Canaria also came from this area and are still visible is Calle de Vegueta in Las Palmas, Gran Canaria.

500 meters north of Ajuy is the small port of Puerto de la Peña which is where Jean de Betencourt and Gadifer le Salle landed in 1402 before moving on and founding the capital of Betancuria. Puerto de la Peña served as the main fishing and trading port of the capital (including the limestone quarried nearby). Puerto de Cabras (now Puerto del Rosario) took

over as the main trading port in the mid 19th Century due to its larger size.

There are a good number of restaurants and cafes in Ajuy. With its fishing background you will often find local island families enjoying fish and seafood meals here at the weekend.

The fine black sand beach is a great place to sunbathe, though swimming in the sea is not advised unless it is a calm day, as the sea can be very rough and there are strong currents. There are, however some small natural pools that fill up with water and are a great place for a dip once the tide has gone out – just follow the locals.

A noted scuba dive site, known as the Cathedral is located just off the coast of Ajuy, though it is only for very advanced divers, due to the rough seas and strong currents. Stunning volcanic rock formations of canals and grottoes, along with overhangs and drop offs make it a great diving location. Rays, Groupers, Barracudas and Angel Sharks are often spotted here amongst the plethora of marine life.

Some 7 km south of Ajuy is Playa de Garcey. This rugged beach used to draw visitors to view the spectacle of the shipwrecked American Star liner that ran aground in 1994 after its tow lines broke during a heavy storm. By 2013, what remained of the wreck (after its original 1940's internal decor was looted by locals), was only visible at low tide and today there is nothing visible.

Final note on the Beach and pools.

Ajuy's beach is ideal to shake off your stress and forget your daily routine. It's where you'll find absolute peace. There are never many people, mainly locals from the area. It has black sand and calm waters. It is definitely recommended as a way to top off a trip to the village.

Less well known, perhaps because they are slightly further away and difficult to find, are the Charcones de Ajuy. One of the village's best-kept secrets. They are small natural pools with crystal-clear waters at the foot of a cliff. The walk up to them is by itself spectacular.

If you go, it is best to do so at low tide, as at high tide bathing can be more difficult. Also, try not to bring too many things, as it isn't an easy task to reach the pools.

AJUY BEACH

AJUY CAVES

WALKWAY ABOVE CAVES

THE SOUTHERN ROUTE

Heading south on the FV-2 out of Caleta de Fuste , for our first stop, Cardon village. A 40 minute and 45.7 km drive.

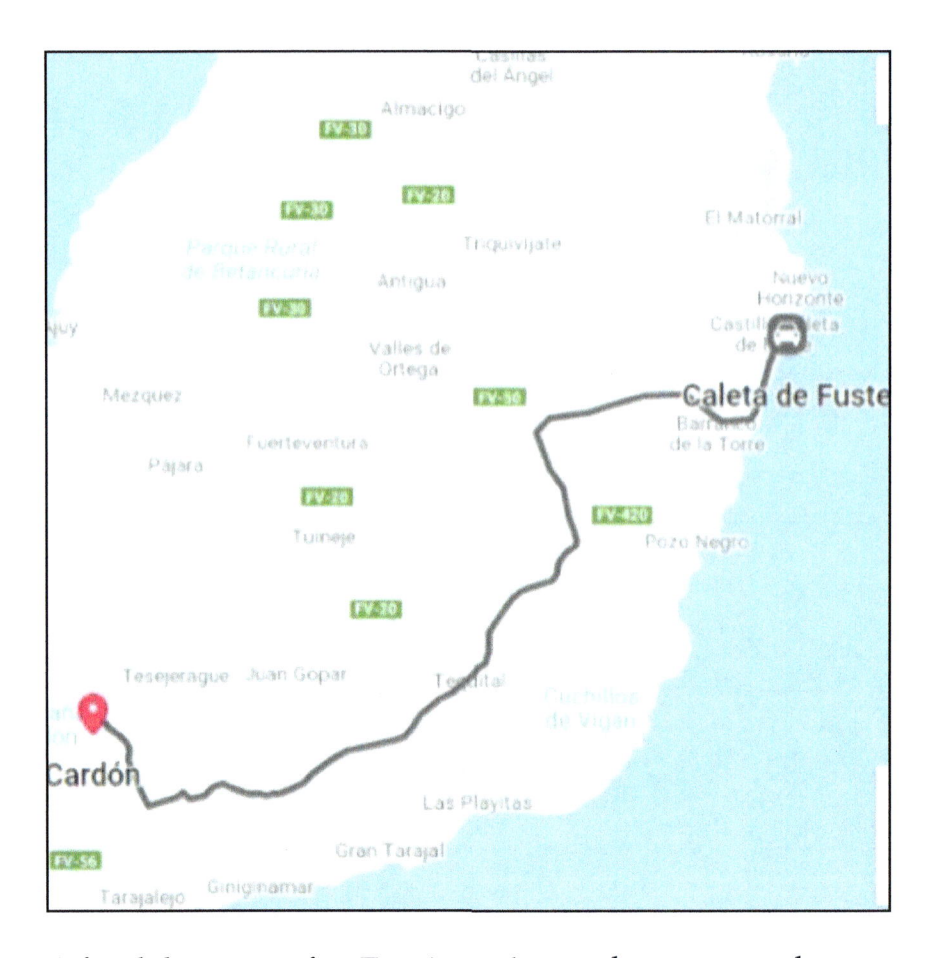

A few kilometers after Teguitar take a right turn onto the FV-511 then the first left onto FV-56, the first right off this road is the FV- 618, heading for the village of Cardón, this is our stopping point as we make our way to Montaña del Cardón.

Parking in Cardón at the church. From the road turn left towards La Tanquita hermitage. Just before the chapel on the right, follow the hill to the road and continue on the left. Turn left at the Chilegua farmhouse, over the next hill (dirt road) to Las Hermosas. Follow the road to the right, on the next hill the path goes to the left back to the start and destination Cardón. Hiking is not difficult, but it does take a bit of fitness. Good footwear is important because the trails sometimes have a lot of rocks.

SR-1 Montaña del Cardón.

The Cardón Mountain Natural Monument is a mountainous massif that was formed by the superposition of volcanic flows that covered part of the Basal Complex (oldest geological unit of the island).

It presents an imposing appearance with its 690 meters high and takes the form of a knife, the result of a continuous erosion of several million years on ancient materials, Its slopes are partially affected by headwaters of narrow valleys, while its summit evolves towards a flat plateau.

The Cardones Mountain in addition to its great natural beauty hides the sacralization of the aborigines. Not only because it was a mountain, since for the majos, some mountains were considered sacred, since they saw them as a link between heaven and earth.

On the other hand, this mountain is accompanied by the legend of Mahan, an aboriginal noble warrior who carried out great feats and heroic acts. According to legend, he was buried in Montaña Cardones, where he was venerated and respected as a hero.

Today the mountain continues to receive faithful, but in this case of Christian belief. At the beginning of the twentieth century, according to popular beliefs, when the excavation of a gallery for the collection of water was carried out, some neighbours of the place distinguished in the rock the figure of the Virgen del Tanquito.

It is from then on when this place began to be venerated by the neighbors to ask for favors and make promises.

Oral tradition tells us that in the seventies of the last century, a neighbour climbed into the gallery a picture of the Virgin, whom they were going to worship. After the time this ritual was gaining followers becoming the current pilgrimage of the Virgen del Tanquito. This image adored by the residents of Cardón moves once a year, from its current location to the place where one day its image appeared.

This pilgrimage is of recent creation, where Canarian folklore meets once a year, and all the parishioners come dressed and dance to the image of the Virgen del Tanquito.

After walking on the trails through Montaña del Cardón, head back to the car for one of the most spectacular viewpoints on the island of Fuerteventura, the viewpoint of Sicasumbre, a viewpoint located at the foot of the Cardón Mountain.

Located in the south of the island of Fuerteventura, in the municipality of Pájara, the viewpoint of Sicasumbre is an excellent point of observation of the sky, having indications on the location of the constellations of stars, a solar clock and a vertical one. For the most experienced amateurs, in the viewpoint of Sicasumbre the necessary supports have been arranged so that the visitor can install their own telescopes and cameras. The night panorama of 3 constellations: Virgo, Boyero and Cuervo are really impressive. From the astronomical viewpoint of Sicasumbre, located about 300 meters above sea level, in the early hours of the night you can see with relative ease a prominent star in early spring; it is Espiga, the main star of the constellation of Virgo. Very close to it is the constellation of the Bouvier, with Arthur as a prominent star, while to the right of Virgo is the small constellation of the Raven, characteristic for its rhombus or quadrilateral shape.

MONTANA DEL CARDON.

Our next journey south to, La Pared, is only a short distance away.

SR-2 La Pared

Only a 13 minute 16.9 km drive and we will arrive in La Pared. La Pared is situated on the wild, rugged and windswept western side of the Jandia Peninsula's isthmus in Southern Fuerteventura. Though the narrow strip of land that separates Costa Calma from La Pared measures just 5 km across (the narrowest point of the Island), the contrast between the two places couldn't be more striking. Set in a dramatic landscape of jagged volcanic mountains, with dark blue foamy waters, La Pared showcases the wild west coast of Fuerteventura. The village is named after the wall (pared is Spanish for wall), that divided the two 'kingdoms' of Maxorata and Jandia which were ruled by indigenous kings.

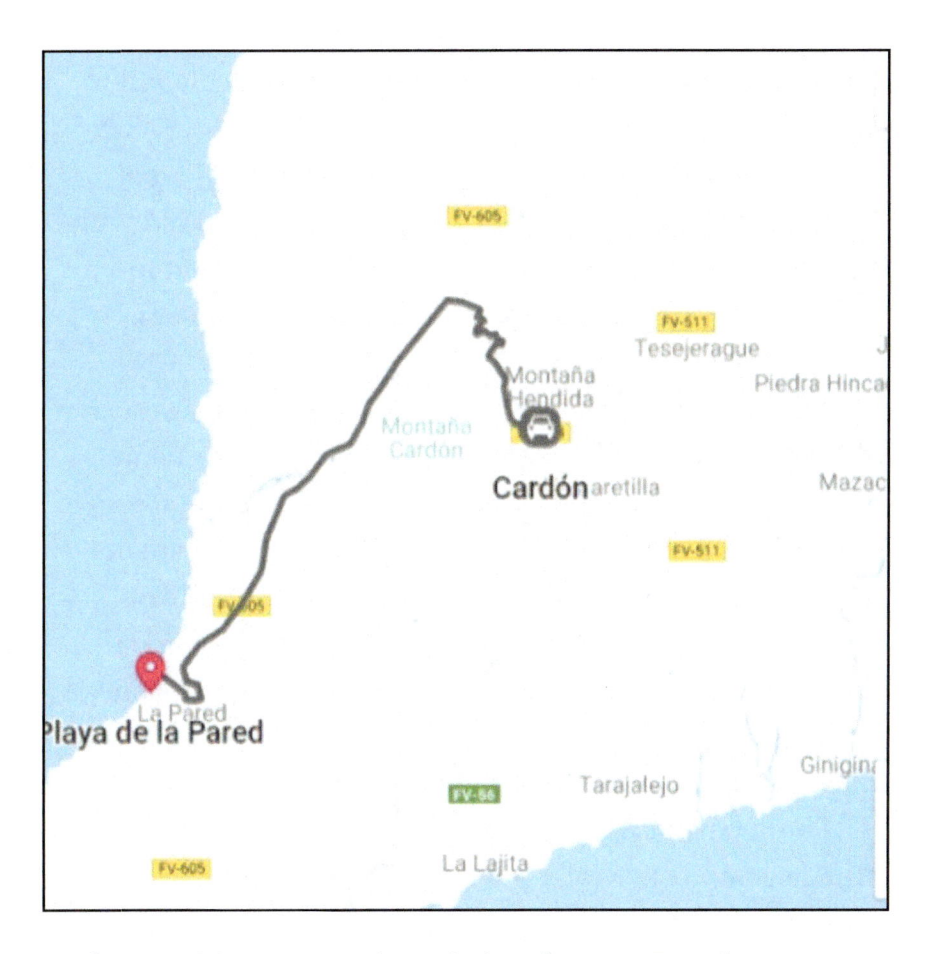

With its wild waters and sandy beaches, La Pared is a great place to learn to surf and there are a number of schools offering classes. The beauty of this dark-sand beach is not to be missed, though the wild waters with strong currents make it unsuitable for swimming. Depending on the wind and surf levels, kite surfing here is possible, although not recommended for beginners. The beach is split in two parts, the smaller of the two, (known as Playa La Pared) is accessed via the steps from the cliff top (in front of the La Pared Hotel) and ends where the rocks reach into the sea. Take a look to your right on the way down for a spectacular view through a lava arch. The second beach, Playa de Viejo Rey, lies to the south and can be accessed via Playa La Pared during low tide or via the cliff-top path that is marked with large stones. It really is a stunning location and great fun to watch all the surfers (if you aren't on a board yourself).

There are no facilities on either of La Pared's beaches, such as toilets, showers, life guards or sun loungers so, ensure you come prepared with water and sun-cream. The access to both beaches is rocky with uneven steps, thus they are not recommended for young children, the elderly or infirm. You will find a few cafes, restaurants and a mini-market here, before dropping down to the beach, though it is only a short 7 km drive into the much larger tourist resort of Costa Calma, if the local amenities don't suffice.
"La Pared powered by Las Playitas", formerly called "Bungalows Costa Real", is the only hotel in the area. It is currently managed by the sporty Las Playitas resort complex, located just outside of Gran Tarajal on the east coast.

There are stables nearby, offering horse riding in the area, a great way to sightsee in and around La Pared, and a small Golf Academy with a short artificial-grass 9-hole course, putting green and driving range, this is more suitable for beginners compared to other courses on the island. Sadly, this Golf Academy has not re-opened and looks to be abandoned (summer 2022). The beaches do get quite busy with surfers in this area, so take extra care if you decide to go for a swim.

PLAYA PARED

1 hour 6 minutes, 50.4 km drive south is our next destination, Playa Cofete.

Taking the FV-605, passing through Costa Calma, Jandia, and Morro Jable, which are all ideal places to stop of for a night and explore the stunning beaches, but for now lets make headway and see the stunning Playa Cofete.

SR-3 Cofete

Cofete is a area of untamed beauty. A 15 kilometer long stretch of wild and remote golden-sand beach, accessed by a single dirt track with barely a building in sight. Cofete is the largest and one of the wildest beaches in the Canary Islands and in my opinion, one of the most spectacular. Apparently I am not alone; Trip Advisor users voted it one of the top 10 European beaches in 2015. Set in the remote south-west of Fuerteventura, Cofete sits within the Jandia Natural Park.

A cliff-like ridge, crowned by the island's highest peak, Pico de la Zarza (806m), towers above Cofete, creating a spectacular backdrop to the miles of sand. The Barlavento (windward) beaches take more of a beating from the Atlantic, especially compared to the eastern side of the island (where the tourist resorts are located). Unlike La Pared to the north, Cofete is not recommended for surfing unless you are very competent and the conditions are right (which isn't often).

Strong currents and high winds mean that this area is not suitable for swimming, even for the strongest of swimmers.

Access to Cofete is via a graded dirt-road or on foot. And while many visitors make this journey in a 'regular' car, most hire companies don't insure you 'off-road', so you could end up paying for a tow-truck out of your own pocket. The dirt-track is generally well-maintained, however its condition does vary throughout the year, so a 4×4 is recommended. A special 4×4 Bus service runs twice a day from the bus station in Morro Jable, however i suggest that you do not rely on it, since it fills up very quickly, i did once try to catch this bus and were turned away, due to it being full. Interestingly, the Mercedes buses used on this route were specially-made for the production of the Ridley Scott Movie, Exodus: Gods and Kings, to ferry extras and crew back and forth, before gaining a new lease of life as local buses in 2014. Please take note of the above if you are in a hire car.

MOST HIRE COMPANIES DON'T INSURE YOU FOR OFF ROAD DRIVING.

Along the road to Cofete is a stunning view point called Roque del Morro, a great place to take a picture and the first of many stunning views of the area. You will need a good comfortable pair of shoes for this next part.

There is a great walk to Cofete which really is worthwhile and you can reward yourself with food and a nice cold glass of beer at the restaurant in Cofete before making the return journey (it's 10km each way). The walk is clearly signposted on the turn-off to Cofete, just before you reach the harbour in Morro Jable. You can also drive a little further, parking either at the cemetery just before the tarmac road stops, or further along the dirt road in a small car park next to a number of small holdings. The walk takes around 2.5 hours each way, including a few breaks, and isn't overly challenging. The route begins with a gentle uphill slope through Gran Valle and a final 15-20 minute assent to degollada de Cofete. The descent down the other side of the ridge to Cofete village takes around 45 minutes (and another 15 minutes to reach the beach).

In 2005, Fuerteventura, in conjunction with the Cape Verde islands, started a loggerhead turtle re-introduction programme. Eggs collected in Cape Verde were buried on Cofete beach and, once hatched, the young turtles were brought to the Morro Jable Turtle Nursery, where they were raised in safety, before being released once they had grown a little larger (giving them a better chance of survival). Unfortunately this has not continued in recent years, as it appears the Fuerteventura government didn't keep its end of an agreement with Cape Verde. However, don't be disheartened, as you can still see rescued turtles at the sanctuary in Morro Jable harbour, where injured turtles are nursed back to health and then released on beaches across the Jandia peninsula, It is also hoped that the first turtles released on the beach a few years ago will now start to return to lay their own eggs on the beach.

Sat alongside the beach, near the car park, is a small desolate cemetery. Small mounds of rock and sun-bleached wooden crosses are partially buried underneath the shifting sands. The graveyard dates back to the early 19th century, when the impoverished residents of the Jandia peninsula were forced to create an improvised burial ground for their dead, since the nearest church (in Pajara) was too far away. Feudal-style land ownership meant that the locals had to bury the corpses in the only common ground available – the seashore. The last internment was in 1956. It's quite an eerie place, a cemetery lost in time.

The small ramshackle village of Cofete consists of around 20 small properties, of various build quality. There is one small restaurant, simply called Restaurante Cofete. I have eaten here twice on my visit to this area, and although you shouldn't expect a gastronomic feast, the food was most welcoming after a long hike. One thing i personally like about this place is that they serve Estrella Damm beer, a nice change from Tropical! Prices are a bit on the high side, it gets busy and the service can be a bit slow, but you are in a spectacular location, so just relax and enjoy the view. Halfway along the beach is a rocky outcrop connected to the main beach by a sand spit, known as El Islote. It's a great view point and photo opportunity as you have the wild Atlantic on either side of you.

I would highly recommend watching the sunset in Cofete. Most people head off well before then, so you are likely to have the beach almost to yourself. The sunset is best viewed during the summer months, as the sun sets over the mountains (rather than the sea) during the winter.

COFETE BEACH

The next place i want to mention is a place called, Puerto de la Cruz. It's a 35 minute 17.3 km drive to the southern tip of Fuerteventura.

WARNING! THIS TRIP IS ONLY ADVISABLE IF YOU ARE DRIVING A 4X4 VEHICLE, AS I MENTIONED BEFORE, A NORMAL HIRE CAR WILL NOT BE INSURED, ON DIRT TRACKS.

SR-4 Puerto de la Cruz

Nestled alongside Puertito de la Cruz, an interesting fishing village in southern Fuerteventura, is Puerto de la Cruz Beach, next to Punta de Jandía lighthouse, also known as Piragua Beach. It is accessible by car via the dirt track leading from the town of Morro Jable.

This is a secluded, virgin beach where visitors are welcome to practise naturism – an almost deserted place in Pájara with charm enough to continue to attract holidaymakers.

Visitors to the beach can enjoy a natural landscape surrounded by white sand, with a hidden reef treasure in its crystalline waters with moderate waves. Care must be taken when swimming off this section of the coast, as undertows and currents are strong. The beach is accessible by off-road car, it is too remote and its surrounding terrain too uneven to come here by ordinary car, but the journey is worth it, as you can enjoy views of the semi-wilderness of the region on your way to the beach.

Puerto de la Cruz Beach is an undiscovered place where tourists can spend an exciting day, perhaps even hiking, and enjoy the area's natural charm. The beach is a must-see for anyone visiting the region in search of adventure.

PUERTO DE LA CRUZ

As i mentioned earlier, a few places we passed on our route to Cofete, are worth a stop off. I would personally choose one for a nights sleep over then explore the stunning beaches on offer, south of the island.

MORRO JABLE BEACH

JANDIA BEACH

SOTAVENTO BEACH COSTA CALMA

Lastly, whilst on our journey back up the FV-2, you may wish to stop off at, La Lajita, (Oasis Park).

SR-5 La Lajita, (Oasis Park).

The major tourist attraction on the island is the Fuerteventura zoo, which is in the south of the island at La Lajita, and is called Oasis Park. It is advertised as the biggest park in the Canary Islands, and offers an extensive zoo with animal shows, a large cactus garden and a large garden centre. It is open 365 days of the year from 9am – 6pm.

The Fuerteventura zoo covers an area of about one million m2, and offers a full day out for anyone who enjoys being with animals and enjoys walking around the enclosures and open areas. There are over 3000 animals from 250 species, and the zoo specializes in animals that live in savannah area. There is also a successful conservation policy.

At the entrance there is a ticket office where you buy your tickets. It is also possible to buy tickets online at the zoo's website, and this offers discounted admission which is valid for 3 months.

TICKET PRICES: OASIS WILDLIFE FUERTEVENTURA

Correct as Summer 2022.

Adult

Ticket From 12 onwards

38,50€

Senior

Entry Over 60 years old

31,50€

Entrance Child

From 4 to 11 years old

23,00€

Entrance Child with disabilities

From 4 to 15 years old

20,50€

Entry Adult with disability

From 16 onwards

31,50€

Infant

Entrance From 0 to 3 years old

0,00€

Motorized scooters are available to hire for those with reduced mobility.

At the Fuerteventura zoo you can see elephants, giraffes, zebras, hippos, cheetahs, camels, crocodiles, alligators, flamingoes, otters, mongoose, tortoises, lemurs, snakes, parrots and birds, raccoons, meerkats, coatis, ostrich, wallabies, lynx and a range of primates, large and small.

Included in the admission price are 4 shows. There are at least 2 shows each day to see the parrots, the reptiles, the sea lions and the birds of prey. All are interactive and entertaining. Within the zoo there is also a petting farm where you can meet a range of farm animals, such as cows, sheep, goats, horses, donkeys etc.

Oasis Park Fuerteventura

OASIS PARK

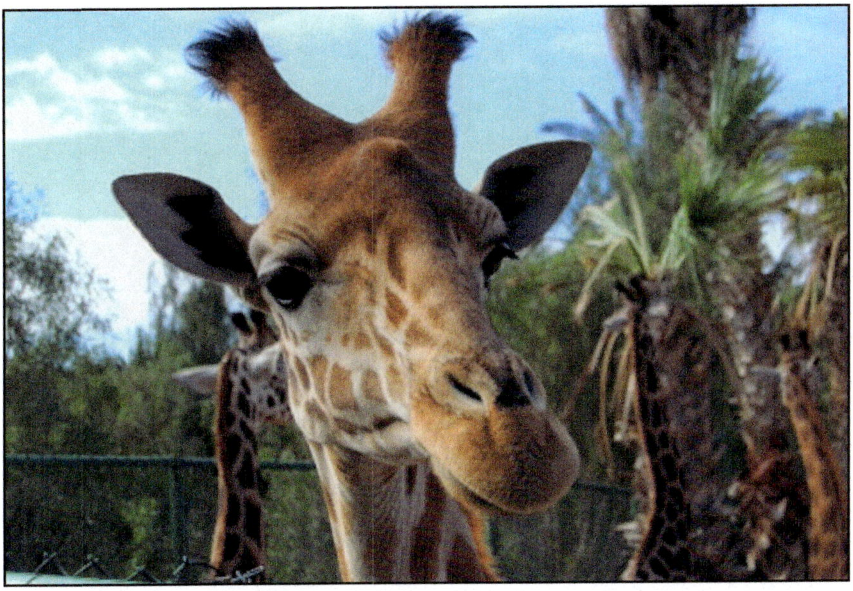

TOURIST MAP

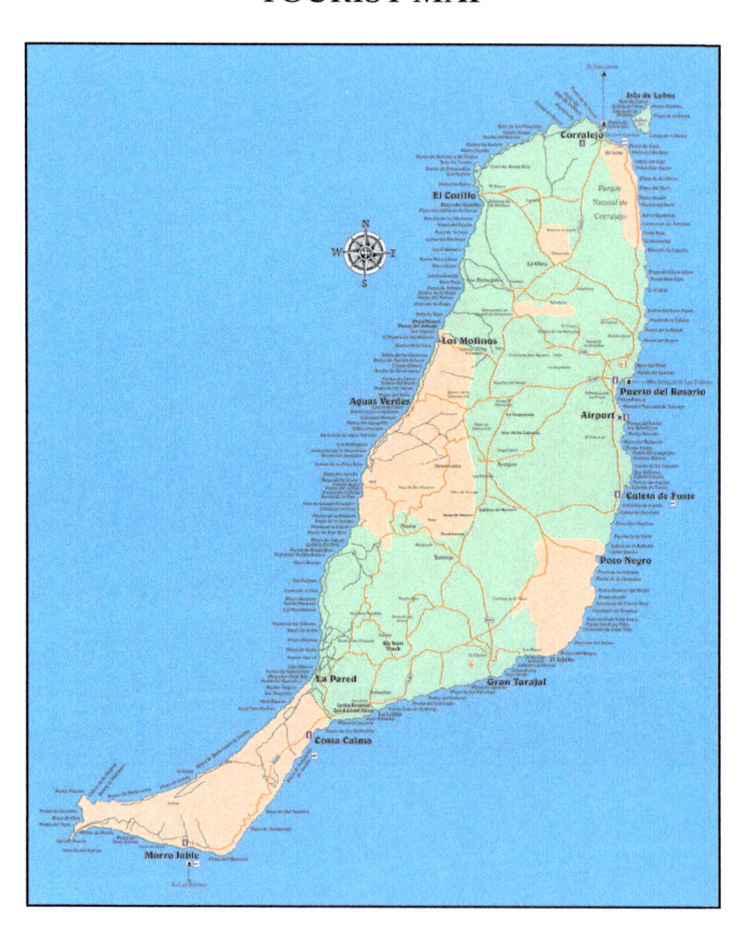

IMPORTANT INFO FOR DRIVING IN SPAIN

What driving licences can you use in Spain?

If you are taking your car, you must find out if your driving licence is valid to drive in Spain, whether you must exchange it or if you need to obtain the International Permit.

Permits issued in countries of the European Union and the European Economic Area (Iceland, Liechtenstein and Norway) are fully valid to drive in Spain as long as they are in force.

If you come from any other country, it is advisable that you get the international permit in your country before you travel. This permit is valid for one year and is complementary. So, whenever you are going to use it, you must also present your passport and your foreign driving license.

More information on other valid permits to drive in Spain.

Also, keep in mind that the minimum driving age in Spain is 18 years old.

Also, remember that it is absolutely necessary to have valid international insurance. If you are a citizen of the European

Union, Switzerland, Norway, Iceland, Liechtenstein, Andorra, Bosnia-Herzegovina, Serbia or Montenegro you'll need to have the insurance policy with you together with the receipt justifying its validity. If you are from Albania, Azerbaijan, Belarus, Iran, Israel, Macedonia, Morocco, Moldavia, Tunisia, Turkey, Ukraine or Russia, you must obtain a Green Card or International Civil Liability Insurance Certificate. For all other cases, it will be necessary to take out Border Insurance.

Since conditions may vary, we suggest that you contact the Spanish Embassy or Consulate to verify these requirements before you start your trip.

How do you rent a car?

To rent a vehicle in Spain, you must be at least 21 years old and have a valid driving licence. Many companies also require you to have had your driving licence for a minimum of one or two years. To complete the car hire process, you will need a credit card.

Remember that if more than one person is going to drive, the others must appear as additional drivers on the contract. Also, the rate tends to be higher for those under the age of 25.
In Spain, it is usual for rental cars to have manual transmission and the rate for those with automatic transmission tend to be higher.

What are the most important rules?

In Spain, we drive on the right, safety belts are mandatory for all the occupants of the vehicle and there are speed limits on all roads. These are 120 km/h on dual carriageways and motorways, 90 km/h on all other roads and 30 km/h in built-up areas.

Other important rules are:

It is forbidden to talk on a mobile phone without a hands-free device or to handle one while driving.

Overtaking can only be done on the left side of the car which you wish to pass.

Children under 135 centimetres in height cannot sit in the front seat and they must always use an approved restraint system. It is recommended to use a restraint system with a back until the child is over 150 centimetres tall. These instructions also apply to taxis, so if you want to travel with a baby in a taxi, you must carry an approved restraint system.

If you drink, don't drive: blood alcohol levels must not exceed 0.5 g/l (0.25 mg/l in exhaled air).

Helmets must be worn on motorbikes, mopeds and bicycles.

Parking in public thoroughfares is not always permitted or free. In many cities the parking areas are regulated and subject to payment. Normally these can be identified by the presence of parking meters in the vicinity.

Which roads have tolls and which do not?

In Spain, the vast majority of roads in the national network are free to use. These include motorways (independent roads in each direction and with no intersections at the same level).

Nevertheless, there is a series of roads that may require the payment of a toll. These are the motorways. The cost varies in each case, but there are generally alternative routes that are free to use.

You can check the highways that require toll payment on this website.

Tolls may be paid in cash, by credit card or using electronic toll services (requires the installation of a device in the car)

What should you do if you get a fine?
Traffic violations sanctioned in the Road Safety Act must always be paid. There are two possibilities when you receive a traffic fine:

If you are informed of the fine when the violation is committed, it can be paid on the spot. If it is not possible to pay it, the Civil Guard may impound the vehicle until it is paid.

If you are informed of the fine by post, you will have various options to pay:

1. Using the telephone number 060 (from Spain): the service is in Spanish only. Payment is made by credit card. From abroad the contact telephone number is: +34 902887060.

2. Online: from the General Directorate of Traffic of Spain

3. In person:

At branches of Caixabank.

In Spanish post offices (Correos de España), paying an additional fee of 1.50% of the amount of the fine.

At Provincial Traffic Offices using a credit or debit card.

Remember: if the fine is paid within 20 calendar days, there is a 50% reduction on the amount of the fine.

IN CASE OF EMERGENCY

Important Telephone Numbers
Teléfonos de Interés
Wichtige Rufnummern
Numéros de téléphone importants
Numeri di telefono
Belangrijke telefoonnummers

Emergency | Urgencia | Notruf | Urgence
Emergenza | Noodgeval: **112**
Guardia Civil: 062 | Policía Local: 092

Policia Local:
Corralejo: +34 928 866 107
Puerto del Rosario: +34 928 850 635
Costa Calma: +34 928 875 175
Jandia/Morro Jable: +34 928 541 020

Health Centre | Centro de Salud
Ärztezentrum
Corralejo: +34 928 535 480
Caleta de Fuste: +34 928 163 926
Costa Calma: +34 928 875 564
Jandia/Morro Jable: +34 928 545 070

Tourist Office | Oficina de Turismo
Fremdenverkehrsamt
Corralejo: +34 928 866 235
Caleta de Fuste: +34 928 163 286
Puerto del Rosario: +34 928 530 844
Costa Calma: +34 928 875 079
Jandia/Morro Jable: +34 928 540 776

Dr. Med. | Medico | Arzt:
Corralejo (Dra. K. Werner): +34 928 537 474
Jandia:
(Centro Medico Jandia): +34 928 541 543

Dentist | Dentista | Zahnarzt:
Corralejo (J. Scharping): +34 928 535 174
Jandia: (B. Pelka): +34 928 541 799

Airport | Aeropuerto | Flughafen:
+34 928 860 500
Hospital Puerto del Rosario:
+34 928 862 000

EXPLORING BY BUS

Two of the most asked questions on the fuerteventura forum pages is :-

Can i get a bus from, (example, Caleta - Corralejo? (YES)

I've forgot to bring my driving license, can i use a photo copy? (NO)

The island of Fuerteventura, even though it is the second largest island in the archipelago is still small enough for you to get around using a combination of local buses, taxis, bicycle and your own feet.
In this Chapter i will address all the transport options available in Fuerteventura so that you can reach the island's most famous places without a car. Also ferry information for those wishing to cross to Lanazote for a day.

Public transport is quite efficient, is air-conditioned and it is comfortable, clean and cheap. All of the buses on the island have a fixed fare system and metered taxi fares don't change with the seasons.

We will start with the local bus service, named TIADHE. They have a fleet of buses in Fuerteventura equipped with the highest safety conditions. All units have air conditioning and emergency exits are properly signposted. In addition, they have individual seat belts in each seat.

Buses connect almost all of the cities and towns on Fuerteventura. All routes generally follow the timetable indicated at the bus stops. In Fuerteventura, a bus is called a "guagua". But if you use the Spanish word "autobuses" you will be understood perfectly. Buses can take you to all the main places and bring you back again.

Tiadhe and it has 18 lines that connect most points on the island. Some lines serve the north of the island and others connect the south. Depending on your destination, you can get a transfer from Fuerteventura airport to anywhere on the island.

For example, bus route 3 takes you from Fuerteventura airport to Puerto del Rosario (the capital), as well as to tourist areas like Caleta de Fuste and Salinas. In contrast, bus route 10 can take you to Puerto del Rosario and Morro Jable Resort on the south side of the island.

Fares

These are cheap and tickets can be bought on board. The cost will depend on the distance travelled. However, there is a card that allows you to get a discount (5%) on the price of the ticket. It usually costs €2 and can be topped up with at least €5. You can buy them at bus stops, in shops and even at newsstands.

01 Puerto del Rosario – Morro Jable 1 h 49 minutes

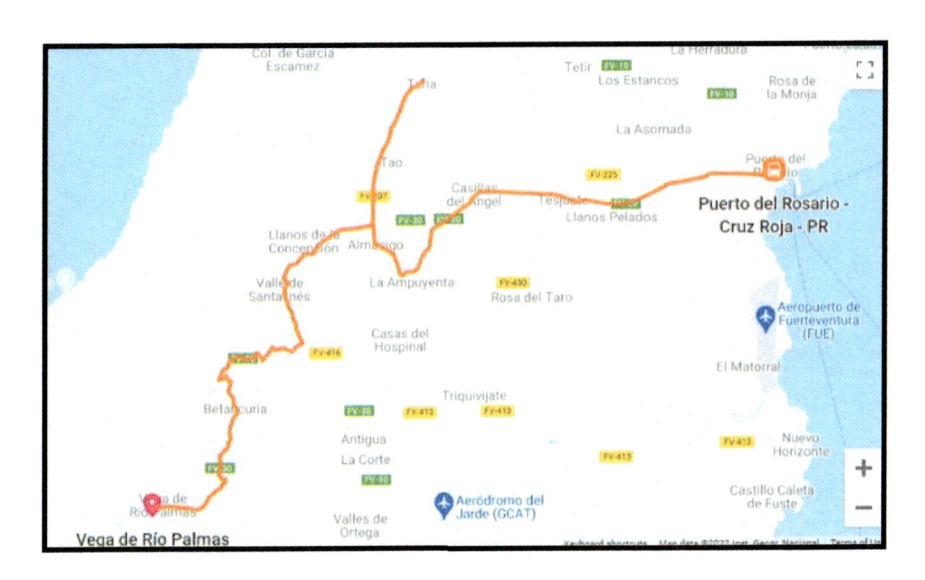

02 Puerto del Rosario – Vega de Río Palmas 59 minutes

03 Puerto del Rosario – Caleta de Fuste – Las Salinas 21 mins

04 Pájara – Morro Jable 59 minutes

05 Costa Calma – Morro Jable 23 minutes

06 Puerto del Rosario – Corralejo 42 minutes

07 Puerto del Rosario – El Cotillo 1 hour

08 Corralejo – El Cotillo 42 minutes

09 Pájara – Morro Jable 59 minutes

10 Puerto del Rosario – Morro Jable (por Pozo Negro) 1h 49 minutes

11 Tuineje – La Lajita – Gran Tarajal 41 minutes

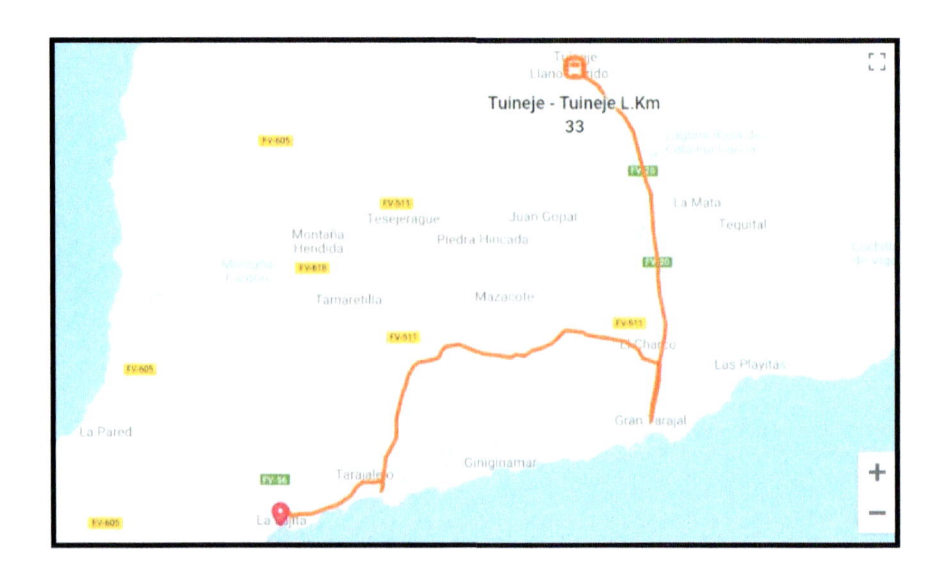

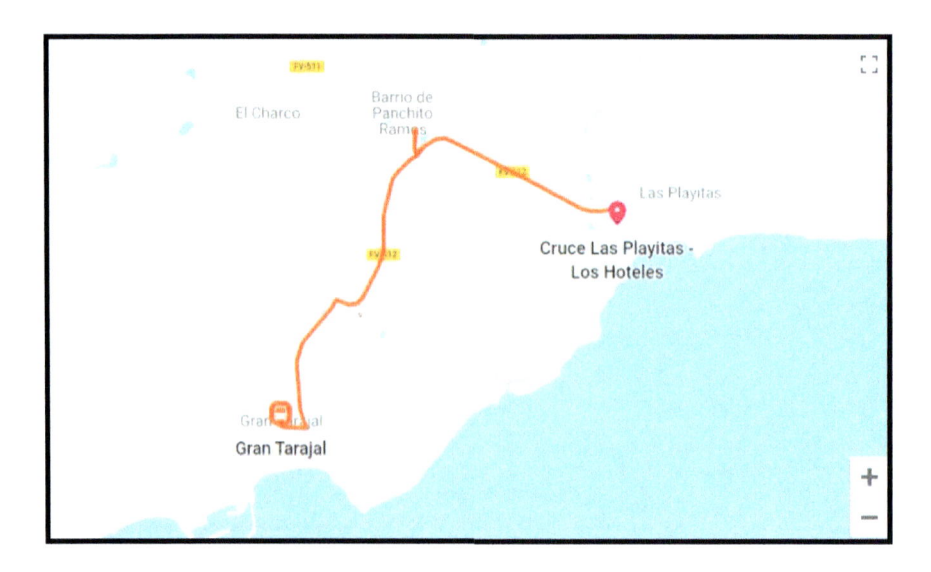

12 Gran Tarajal – Las Playitas 13 minutes

14 Puerto del Rosario – El Time 15 minutes

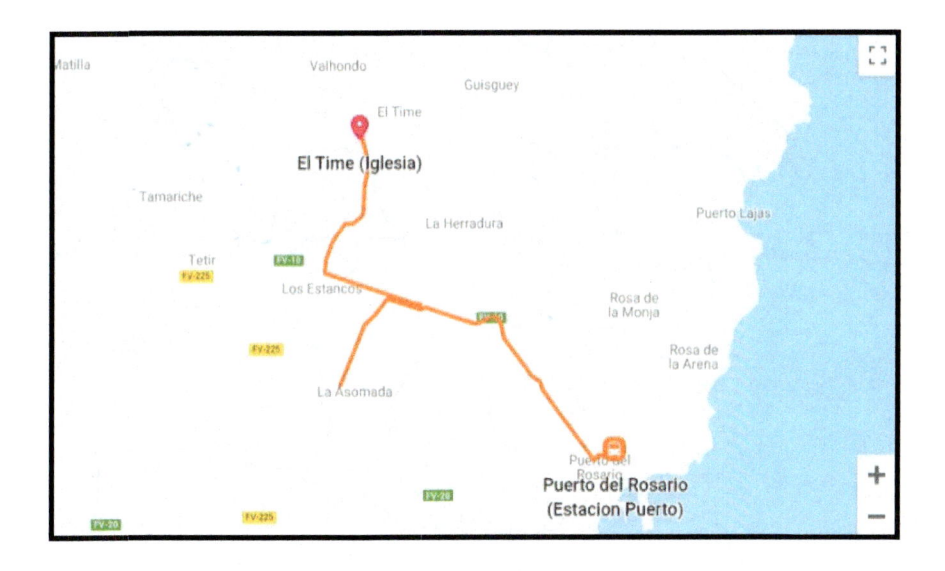

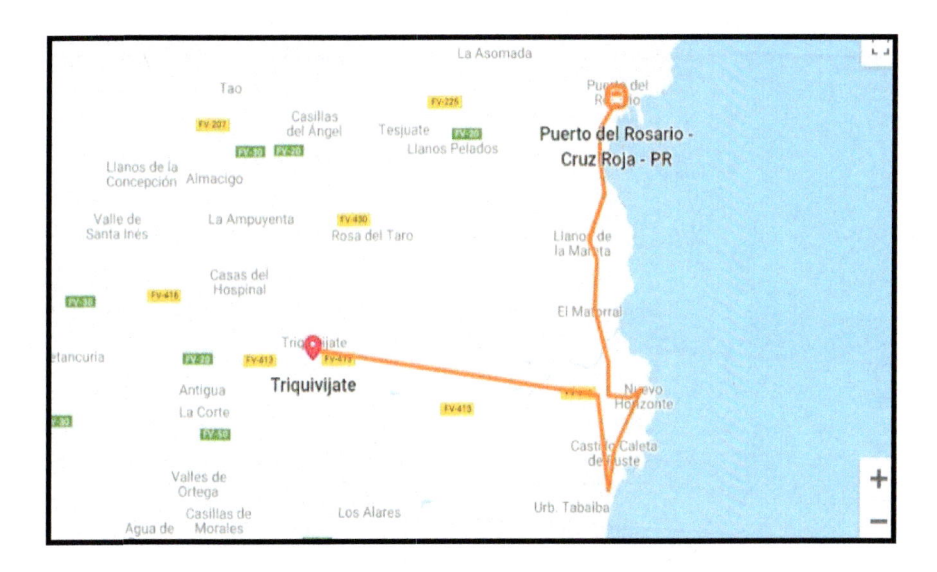

15 Puerto del Rosario – Triquivijate 37 minutes

16 Gran Tarajal – Puerto del Rosario 58 minutes

18 Pájara – Gran Tarajal 28 minutes

25 La Lajita – Morro Jable 35 minutes

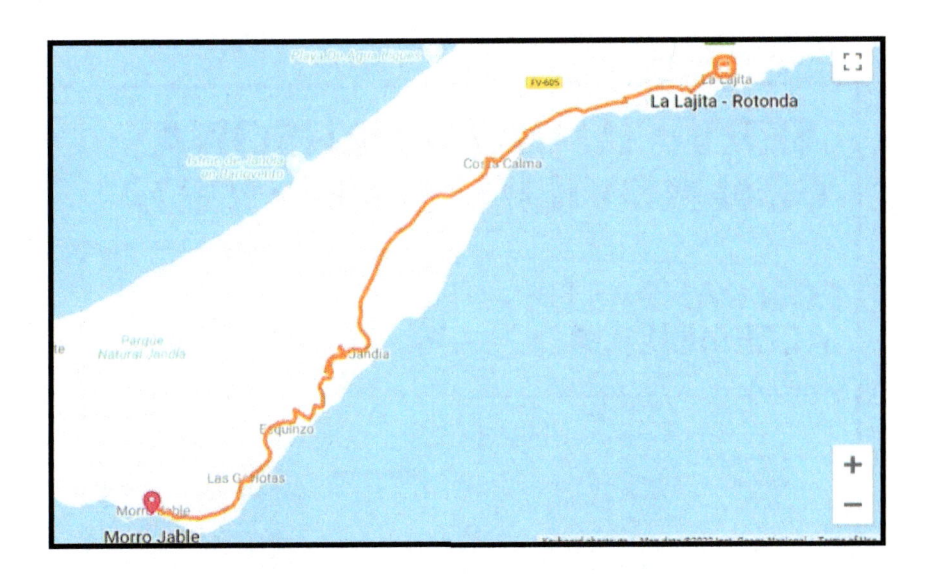

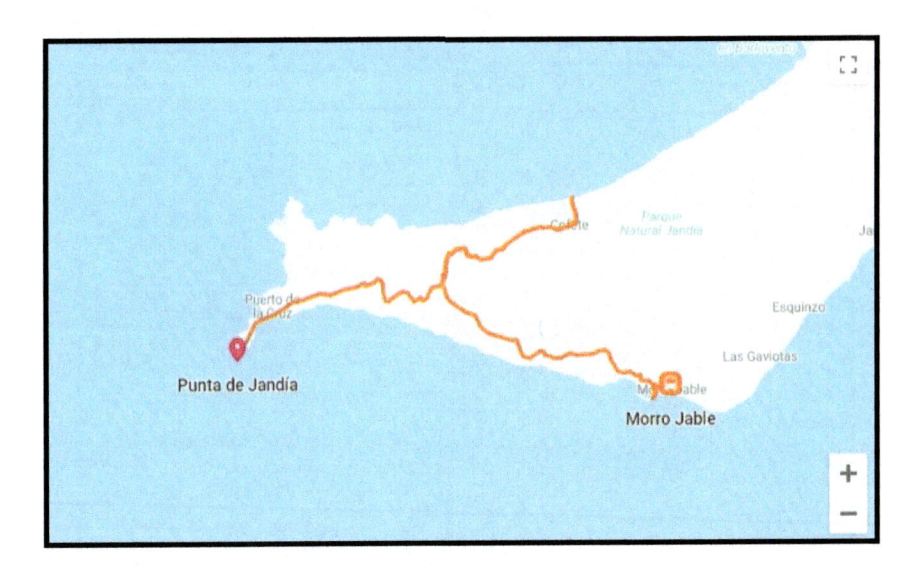

111 Línea Morro Jable – Cofete – Punta de Jandia 37 minutes

Tiadhe, also provide bus services with wheelchair access, time table and routes below.

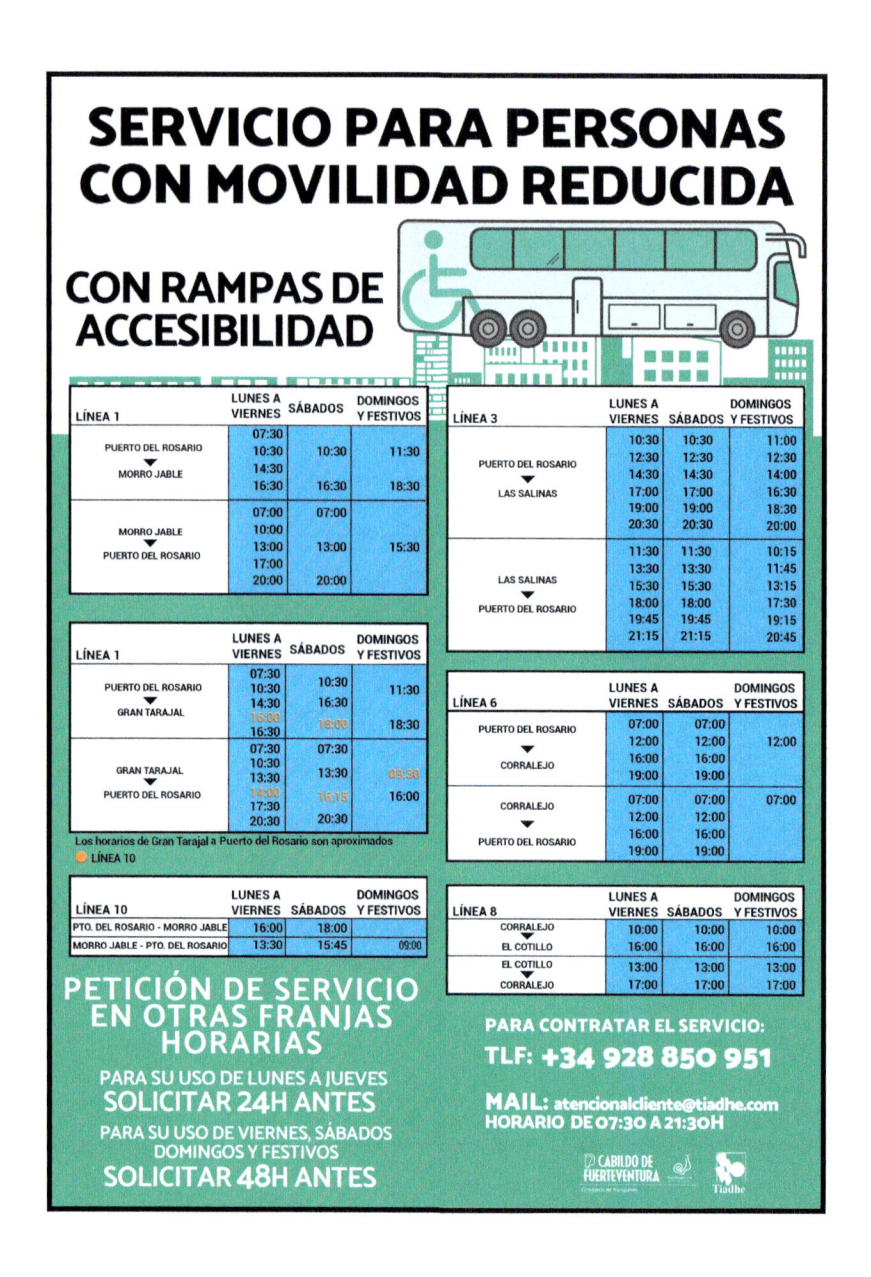

SERVICIO PARA PERSONAS CON MOVILIDAD REDUCIDA

CON RAMPAS DE ACCESIBILIDAD

LÍNEA 1	LUNES A VIERNES	SÁBADOS	DOMINGOS Y FESTIVOS
PUERTO DEL ROSARIO ▼ MORRO JABLE	07:30 10:30 14:30 16:30	10:30 16:30	11:30 18:30
MORRO JABLE ▼ PUERTO DEL ROSARIO	07:00 10:00 13:00 17:00 20:00	07:00 13:00 20:00	15:30

LÍNEA 1	LUNES A VIERNES	SÁBADOS	DOMINGOS Y FESTIVOS
PUERTO DEL ROSARIO ▼ GRAN TARAJAL	07:30 10:30 14:30 15:00 16:30	10:30 16:30 18:00	11:30 18:30
GRAN TARAJAL ▼ PUERTO DEL ROSARIO	07:30 10:30 13:30 14:00 17:30 20:30	07:30 13:30 16:15 20:30	09:30 16:00

Los horarios de Gran Tarajal a Puerto del Rosario son aproximados
● LÍNEA 10

LÍNEA 10	LUNES A VIERNES	SÁBADOS	DOMINGOS Y FESTIVOS
PTO. DEL ROSARIO - MORRO JABLE	16:00	18:00	
MORRO JABLE - PTO. DEL ROSARIO	13:30	15:45	09:00

LÍNEA 3	LUNES A VIERNES	SÁBADOS	DOMINGOS Y FESTIVOS
PUERTO DEL ROSARIO ▼ LAS SALINAS	10:30 12:30 14:30 17:00 19:00 20:30	10:30 12:30 14:30 17:00 19:00 20:30	11:00 12:30 14:00 16:30 18:30 20:00
LAS SALINAS ▼ PUERTO DEL ROSARIO	11:30 13:30 15:30 18:00 19:45 21:15	11:30 13:30 15:30 18:00 19:45 21:15	10:15 11:45 13:15 17:30 19:15 20:45

LÍNEA 6	LUNES A VIERNES	SÁBADOS	DOMINGOS Y FESTIVOS
PUERTO DEL ROSARIO ▼ CORRALEJO	07:00 12:00 16:00 19:00	07:00 12:00 16:00 19:00	12:00
CORRALEJO ▼ PUERTO DEL ROSARIO	07:00 12:00 16:00 19:00	07:00 12:00 16:00 19:00	07:00

LÍNEA 8	LUNES A VIERNES	SÁBADOS	DOMINGOS Y FESTIVOS
CORRALEJO ▼ EL COTILLO	10:00 16:00	10:00 16:00	10:00 16:00
EL COTILLO ▼ CORRALEJO	13:00 17:00	13:00 17:00	13:00 17:00

PETICIÓN DE SERVICIO EN OTRAS FRANJAS HORARIAS

PARA SU USO DE LUNES A JUEVES
SOLICITAR 24H ANTES

PARA SU USO DE VIERNES, SÁBADOS DOMINGOS Y FESTIVOS
SOLICITAR 48H ANTES

PARA CONTRATAR EL SERVICIO:
TLF: +34 928 850 951

MAIL: atencionalcliente@tiadhe.com
HORARIO DE 07:30 A 21:30H

CABILDO DE FUERTEVENTURA — Tiadhe

This chart is in Spanish, here's the translation:-

Lunes A Viernes = Monday to Friday

Sabado = Saturday

Domingos Y Festivos = Sundays & Holidays.

You can also call on the number provided for all other enquires.

FERRY FROM FUERTEVENTURA TO LANZAROTE

How about visting a second Canary Island during your stay? Even an island as beautiful as Fuerteventura can leave you wanting to explore a little further so why not take advantage of the regular ferry companies to the neighbouring island of Lanzarote? Fuerteventura is the second largest of the Spanish Canary Islands, while Lanzarote is the fourth largest and at the northernmost and easternmost point of the archipelago, meaning it is the closest to the African coastline at a distance of 70 miles approximately.

There is only one ferry route travelling between Fuerteventura and Lanzarote. This leaves Corralejo for Playa Blanca, in Lanzarote, time for the sailing is around 25 minutes. Times can vary due to weather situations or demand, so should be checked in advance of any travel plans.

Fuerteventura Lanzarote Ferry Price

Age   One Way   Return

Adult (> 13)   18 €   35 €

Child (3 – 12) 9 €   18 €

Infant (0 – 2) Free   Free

Days & Time

Lanzarote ferry from Fuerteventura is departing everyday at 10:30 am, 1:30 pm, 5:30 pm and 7:30 pm.

Q & A

How much is Ferry tickets from Fuerteventura to Lanzarote in 2022?

Price of Ferry from Fuerteventura to Lanzarote in 2022 – for adults – 18 €; for children between 3-12 years old – 9 €, Infants are free of charge.

How late can I buy my ticket?

You can purchase an online ticket upto 1.5 hours before the ships departure time.

What time should I board?

As a general rule foot passengers should be ready to board at least 20 minutes before departure time.

Is smoking allowed on board?

No, it is standard procedure that no smoking is permitted aboard any of the fleet.

Is there anything for kids onboard?

Yes. They can use one of the designated play areas or for the older children they can access the onbaord entertainment available online.

Can I purchase food and drinks onboard?

Yes, there are cafes and restaurant services available on the ship.

AUTHOR NOTE

Thank you for reading"Fuerteventura road trip". This book is the second one to follow on from my first book of this island, titled "Fuerteventura". It took me months upon months to write the first book, mostly because i changed the manuscript so many times. In the first book i wrote about the places i recommended to stay whist on the island, "My top 5", even though i included a brief chapter called "off the beaten track" i still thought there was more to write about, hence the birth of "Fuerteventura road trip".

After living on the Island for a number of years i put together all the places i had personally visited knowing how much i had enjoyed them and was totally stunned from such beauty the island of Fuerteventura has to offer, i felt it was my duty to tell everyone about the hidden gems in Fuerteventura, and where to find them.

Being a amateur photographer i also kept lots of notes along side all the photos i had taken which helped when putting this book together. I knew i would write these books on Fuerteventura back in the early 2000's and notes were being taken daily, from the early days, the problem was, back in those days i was so busy with the running of my other businesses, the writing was put to one side, so you can say the first book on Fuerteventura actually took me years to complete.

After leaving the Island in 2014 i once again picked up a pen and began to share this journey with you, but i got side tracked by other thoughts racing through my mind, "how did i get to Fuerteventura"? when did this journey begin? This was the start of first book "it's given when you ask". This tells the story from 1976 when i made myself homeless and set of on a journey searching for my dream, my paradise, all the struggles i faced along the way, but gratitude and the law of attraction led me to my goal. So you see i felt i couldn't write any books on Fuerteventura without me telling the story of how i got there, i needed to tell my story, my ups and downs, my heartache, i needed to do it for me, regardless of how many copies i would sell, this was my book, my journey and the start of a love for writing. Today i have around 29 books published, all non fiction, including a series of 4 books on Ho'oponopono, law of attraction, some journals and notebooks. I am now fully retired and living in northern Thailand with my second wife. My days are taken up with writing new drafts for book ideas and the odd days gardening.

There will be another book on Fuerteventura, a true story on as i call them "the crazy gang of 2001", It's complicated so many people involved, sadly a few-are no longer with us, i'm in the early stages of putting a draft together.

Being a Author is a SMALL BUSINESS, a difficult and time consuming job, a lot of us writers rely on reviews to help our work get noticed. Amazon for instance will list books in it's newsletters and other free promotions after 50 reviews. Every review i receive i personally read, good average. or bad, each review helps me improve on my work and lets me know what the reader wants. If you enjoyed reading this book, and you would like to leave a review, please follow the link below.

https:www.amazon.co.uk/review/create-review?&asin=B0BD5H14ZC. Once again thank you.

References

Transportes Antonio Díaz Hernández, S.L.
Carretera del Sur Km. 3,7 (Zurita)
35600, Puerto del Rosario
Fuerteventura.

Fred. Olsen Cruise Lines, Fred. Olsen House, White House Rd, Ipswich, Suffolk, IP1 5LL

Google maps.

Notes from Favorite trips.

Notes on Favorite trips.

Notes on Favorite trips.

Notes on Favorite trips.

Printed in Great Britain
by Amazon